Summer Cocktails

A Well-Stocked Bar

Before you worry about going out and breaking the bank to make every drink in this book, I would highly recommend reading through the whole thing and picking the cocktails that excite you the most. That way you can focus on buying two or three bottles of liquor that you know you're going to use, rather than having a bunch of bottles with an ounce or two missing that sit on your shelf for months.

The essentials:

- Three bottles of your preferred spirits.

- Simple syrup. Make your own by combining one part sugar (I prefer Demerara sugar for my simple syrup) to one part boiling water. Just stir the water and sugar until the sugar has fully dissolved.

- Fresh fruits. Particularly citrus fruits. You'll notice many of the recipes in this book use lemon and lime juice. Be sure to wash your fruits before using them as garnish.

- A cocktail shaker. No need to get fancy with this one. I use a $2 plastic cocktail shaker I found in a thrift shop that works great. For the drinks that require a mixing glass, you can use the cup part of your cocktail shaker.

- A mixing spoon. It's probably worth getting a nice spoon with an extra long stem, as it tells people you know what you're doing.

- Bitters. No bar is complete without bitters. Start with Angostura bitters as they work universally in every cocktail. Be on the look out for new and interesting bitters too. Bitters last a long time, and they really go a long way in making any cocktail that much better.

Contents

Kalimotxo 7
Toronto 9
Butterscotch & Rum Milkshake 11
Rye Old Fashioned (The Standard) 13
Bourbon Cherry Old Fashioned 15
Tequila Old Fashioned 17
Simple Margarita 19
Painkiller 21
Classic Daiquiri 23
White Russian 25
The Perfect Rye & Ginger 27
The Gin & Tonic Made Better 29
Paloma 33
Aperol Spritz 35
Lynchburg Lemonade 37
Whiskey Smash 39
Boulevardier 41
Paper Plane 43
Gin Fizz 45
Tom Collins 47
Bloody Maria 49
Chilled Gin & Lillet Martini 51
Sidecar 53
Sazerac 55
Mai Tai 57
Dark & Stormy 59
Sake Mojito 61
Vermouth Royale 63
Whiskey in a Teacup 65
New York Sour 67
Brown Derby 69
Blood & Sand 71
Corpse Reviver No.1 73
Rob Roy 75
The Sofia 77
Coconut & Rye Whiskey Soda 79

Photos are for inspiration only.

Kalimotxo

I prefer to use a Malbec or a Tempranillo for the wine in this recipe. Don't spend more than $12 on the wine here. For the cola, I like to use cane sugar cola.

Serving Size

Makes 1 drink

Ingredients

4 oz red wine

4 oz cola

1 orange slice for garnishing

Directions

Pour red wine into a tall glass filled with ice. Top off glass with cola. Stir gently and garnish with orange slice.

Toronto

Serving Size
Makes 1 drink

Ingredients
2 oz Canadian rye whiskey

1/2 oz Fernet-Branca fernet

2 dashes Angostura bitters

1/4 oz Canadian maple syrup

1 lemon peel for garnishing

Directions
Combine whiskey, fernet, bitters, and maple syrup in a mixing glass with ice and stir for 30 seconds. Strain and pour the cocktail into a serving glass. Cut a small slice in the lemon peel and place it on rim of the glass.

Butterscotch & Rum Milkshake

Serving Size
Makes 1 drink

Ingredients
2 oz dark rum

1 Tbsp butterscotch

3 scoops vanilla ice cream

1/2 tsp ground nutmeg

1/2 tsp ground cinnamon, plus extra for garnishing

Directions
Combine rum, butterscotch, ice cream, nutmeg, and 1/2 tsp ground cinnamon into the bowl of a blender. Blend for 30 seconds, or until fully incorporated. Pour into a parfait glass and garnish with a pinch of ground cinnamon.

Rye Old Fashioned (The Standard)

Serving Size

Makes 1 drink

Ingredients

2 oz Canadian rye whiskey

1/4 oz simple syrup

2 dashes Angostura bitters

1 orange peel for garnishing

Directions

Combine whiskey, simple syrup, and bitters in a mixing glass with ice. Stir for 30 seconds. Rub the orange peel over the edge of a serving glass and place a large ice cube in the glass. Strain and pour the cocktail into the serving glass and garnish with the orange peel.

Bourbon Cherry Old Fashioned

Also known as The Pulse Up.

Serving Size
Makes 1 drink

Ingredients
2 oz bourbon

1/2 oz maraschino cherry syrup

2 dashes Angostura bitters

1 maraschino cherry for garnishing

Directions
Combine bourbon, cherry syrup, and bitters in a mixing glass. Stir for 30 seconds. Strain and pour the cocktail over a large ice cube in a serving glass. Drop maraschino cherry in the glass to enjoy at the bottom of the cocktail.

Tequila Old Fashioned

Serving Size
Makes 1 drink

Ingredients
2 oz reposado tequila

1/4 oz agave syrup

1/4 oz freshly squeezed lime juice

2 dashes Angostura bitters

For the Rim
1 lime wedge

1 tsp kosher salt

1/2 tsp white sugar

1/2 tsp chili powder

Directions
Combine tequila, agave syrup, lime juice, and bitters in a mixing glass with ice. Stir for 30 seconds. Rub the rim of a serving glass with the lime wedge. Mix salt, sugar, and chili powder in a shallow dish and lightly dip the rim of the serving glass into the salt mixture. Strain and pour the cocktail over fresh ice in the serving glass.

Simple Margarita

Serving Size
Makes 1 drink

Ingredients
2 oz añejo or blanco tequila

4 Tbsp freshly squeezed lime juice

1/2 oz agave syrup

For the Rim
1 lime wedge

1 Tbsp kosher salt

Directions
Combine tequila, lime juice, and agave syrup in a cocktail shaker with ice. Shake vigorously for at least 30 seconds. Rub the rim of a serving glass with the lime wedge. Add the kosher salt to a shallow dish and dip the rim of the serving glass into the salt. Strain and pour the cocktail into the serving glass over fresh ice and garnish with the lime wedge.

Painkiller

Serving Size
Makes 1 drink

Ingredients
2 oz Navy style rum

1/2 cup pineapple juice

1 oz freshly squeezed orange juice

1 oz cream of coconut

pineapple wedge for garnishing

grated nutmeg for garnishing (optional)

Directions
Combine rum, pineapple juice, orange juice, and cream of coconut in a cocktail shaker with ice. Shake vigorously. Fill the most tropical glass you have with crushed ice. Strain and pour the cocktail into the glass and garnish with the pineapple wedge and nutmeg.

Classic Daiquiri

Serving Size
Makes 1 drink

Ingredients
2 oz blanco or plata rum

1 oz freshly squeezed lime juice

1 1/2 Tbsp simple syrup

mint leaf for garnishing

Directions
Combine rum, lime juice, and simple syrup in a cocktail shaker with ice. Shake vigorously for 30 seconds. Strain and pour the cocktail into a serving glass and garnish with a mint leaf.

White Russian

Serving Size
Makes 1 drink

Ingredients
2 oz vodka

1 oz Kahlúa

3/4 oz heavy cream

Directions
Pour vodka and Kahlúa over ice in a rocks glass. Top with heavy cream. Stir gently if you would like the cream to incorporate with the liquor, or leave as is.

The Perfect Rye & Ginger

Serving Size
Makes 1 drink

Ingredients
4 oz ginger ale

2 oz Canadian rye whiskey

1 orange slice for garnishing

Directions
Fill a tall (8 or 12 oz) glass with ice. Pour a splash of ginger ale into the bottom of glass to preserve the carbonation in the drink. Pour in whiskey and top with remaining ginger ale. Very gently stir to mix ingredients and garnish with an orange slice.

The Gin & Tonic Made Better

Rosemary

Serving Size

Makes 1 drink

Ingredients

1 sprig rosemary

1 1/2 oz London dry gin

4 oz tonic water

Directions

Fill a rocks glass with ice. Place rosemary sprig upright in the glass. Pour in gin and top with tonic water.

Black Pepper & Cucumber

Serving Size

Makes 1 drink

Ingredients

1 cucumber slice

freshly cracked black pepper

1 1/2 oz London dry gin

4 oz tonic water

Directions

Place cucumber slice in the bottom of a tall glass. Gently muddle cucumber with the bottom of a wooden spoon. Fill the glass with ice and garnish with a pinch of pepper. Pour in gin and top with tonic water. Gently stir to mix ingredients.

The Gin & Tonic Made Better *(cont.)*

Mint & Lime

Serving Size
Makes 1 drink

Ingredients
2 mint leaves

1 lime wedge

1 1/2 oz London dry gin

4 oz tonic water

Directions
Place 1 mint leaf in the palm of your hand and smack it with the palm of your other hand, like you are clapping. Place the crushed mint in the bottom of a tall glass. Squeeze the lime wedge over the mint. Fill glass with ice. Pour gin in the glass and top with tonic water. Garnish with remaining mint leaf.

Paloma

Serving Size
Makes 2 drinks

Ingredients
2 oz tequila

6 oz Mexican grapefruit soda

2 grapefruit slices for garnishing

Directions
Fill 2 tall glasses with 1 oz tequila each and top each with 3 oz Mexican grapefruit soda. Garnish each with a grapefruit slice.

Aperol Spritz

Serving Size
Makes 1 drink

Ingredients
1 1/2 oz Aperol

2 oz Prosecco

2 oz soda water

1 orange slice for garnishing

Directions
Fill half a large stemmed wine glass with ice. Pour Aperol and Prosecco into the glass. Top with soda water and garnish with an orange slice.

Lynchburg Lemonade

Serving Size
Makes 1 drink

Ingredients
1 1/2 oz Tennessee whiskey

1/2 oz triple sec

4 oz freshly squeezed lemon juice

4 oz soda water

1 lemon slice for garnishing

Directions
Fill a pint glass with ice. Pour whiskey and triple sec over the ice. Add lemon juice and soda water. Stir gently to mix ingredients and garnish with a lemon slice.

Whiskey Smash

Serving Size
Makes 1 drink

Ingredients
2 oz bourbon

3 oz freshly squeezed lemon juice

1/2 oz simple syrup

4 mint leaves

1 lemon slice for garnishing

Directions
Fill a cocktail shaker halfway with ice. Pour in bourbon, lemon juice, simple syrup, and add 3 mint leaves. Shake vigorously for 30 seconds. Strain and pour the cocktail into a serving glass over fresh ice. Garnish with remaining mint leaf and a lemon slice.

Boulevardier

Serving Size

Makes 1 drink

Ingredients

1 oz bourbon

1 oz red vermouth

1 oz Campari

orange peel for garnishing

Directions

Combine bourbon, red vermouth, and Campari in a mixing glass with ice. Stir for 30 seconds. Rub a serving glass with the orange peel. Strain and pour the cocktail into the serving glass and garnish with the orange peel.

Paper Plane

Serving Size
Makes 1 drink

Ingredients
1 oz bourbon

1 oz amaro

1 oz Aperol

1 oz freshly squeezed lemon juice

lemon peel for garnishing

Directions
Combine bourbon, amaro, Aperol, and lemon juice in a cocktail shaker with ice. Shake vigorously for 30 seconds. Strain and pour the cocktail into a stemmed serving glass. Fold lemon peel to resemble a paper plane and cut a small slice in middle. Garnish glass with the lemon peel plane on the rim.

Gin Fizz

Serving Size
Makes 1 drink

Ingredients
2 oz gin

1 egg white

1/2 oz simple syrup

1 oz freshly squeezed lemon juice

1 oz soda water

Directions
Combine gin, egg white, simple syrup, and lemon juice in a cocktail shaker and shake vigorously for 30 seconds. Add ice to the cocktail shaker and shake for an additional 30 seconds. Strain and pour the cocktail into a serving glass. Top cocktail with soda water.

Tom Collins

Serving Size
Makes 1 drink

Ingredients
2 oz London dry gin

1/2 oz simple syrup

6 oz freshly squeezed lemon juice

2 oz soda water

1 lemon slice for garnishing

1 maraschino cherry for garnishing

Directions
Fill a large glass with ice. Pour gin, simple syrup, and lemon juice into the glass. Top with soda water and stir gently to mix ingredients. Garnish with a lemon slice and maraschino cherry.

Bloody Maria

Feel free to use more or less hot sauce depending on your spice preferences.

Serving Size
Makes 1 drink

Ingredients
2 oz tequila

5 oz tomato juice

1/2 oz lemon juice

pinch of kosher salt

pinch of pepper

1 tsp Mexican hot sauce

1 tsp Worcestershire sauce

3 pickled jalapeño pepper slices for garnishing

2 tortilla chips for garnishing

For the Rim
1 lime wedge

1 Tbsp kosher salt

Directions
Combine tequila, tomato juice, lemon juice, 1 pinch kosher salt, pepper, hot sauce, and Worcestershire sauce in a cocktail shaker with ice. Shake vigorously for 30 seconds. Rub the lime wedge around the rim of a large serving glass. Add 1 Tbsp kosher salt to a shallow dish and dip the rim of the serving glass into the salt. Strain and pour the cocktail into the serving glass with fresh ice. Garnish with jalapeño pepper slices, lime wedge, and tortilla chips.

Chilled Gin & Lillet Martini

This cocktail requires the gin and Lillet to be extremely cold, so store them in the freezer for 24 hours ahead of time.

Serving Size
Makes 1 drink

Ingredients
1 oz London dry gin

1 oz Lillet

lemon peel for garnishing

Directions
Combine gin and Lillet in a mixing glass and stir for 30 seconds. Strain and pour the cocktail into a serving glass. Garnish with a lemon peel.

Sidecar

Serving Size

Makes 1 drink

Ingredients

2 oz cognac

3/4 oz freshly squeezed lemon juice

3/4 oz triple sec

orange peel for garnishing

Directions

Combine cognac, lemon juice, and triple sec in a cocktail shaker with ice. Shake vigorously for 30 seconds. Rub orange peel around the rim and inside of a serving glass to give the cocktail a pleasant aromatic note. Cut a small slice in the middle of orange peel. Strain and pour the cocktail into the glass. Garnish the glass with the orange peel, resting the peel with the slice on the rim.

Sazerac

Serving Size
Makes 1 drink

Ingredients
1/4 oz absinthe
2 oz rye whiskey
1/2 oz simple syrup
3-4 dashes aromatic or Angostura bitters
1 lemon slice for garnishing

Directions
Fill a serving glass with crushed ice and pour absinthe over the ice. Combine whiskey, simple syrup, and bitters in a mixing glass with ice. Stir for 30 seconds. Dispose of the ice and absinthe in the serving glass. Strain and pour the cocktail into the same serving glass. Skewer the top of the lemon slice with a cocktail pick (if you have one) and rest it on top of the glass so the bottom of the lemon slice touches the drink.

Mai Tai

You can substitute the orgeat syrup with amaretto or almond flavored syrup.

Serving Size
Makes 1 drink

Ingredients
1 1/2 oz light rum (white or amber rum)

1 oz freshly squeezed pineapple juice

1/2 oz triple sec

1/2 oz freshly squeezed lime juice

1/2 oz orgeat syrup

1 oz dark rum

1 pineapple wedge for garnishing

1 maraschino cherry for garnishing

Directions
Combine light rum, pineapple juice, triple sec, lime juice, and orgeat syrup in a cocktail shaker with crushed ice. Shake vigorously for 30 to 60 seconds. Strain and pour the cocktail into a serving glass filled with fresh crushed ice. Top drink with dark rum. Garnish with a pineapple wedge and maraschino cherry.

Dark & Stormy

Serving Size
Makes 1 drink

Ingredients
4 oz ginger beer

2 dashes Angostura bitters

2 oz dark rum

1 lime wedge for garnishing

Directions
Fill a tall glass with ice. Pour ginger beer over the ice and add bitters. Top with dark rum. Spear a lime wedge with a cocktail pick (if you have one) and place over top of the glass for garnish.

Sake Mojito

Serving Size
Makes 1 drink

Ingredients
1/2 oz simple syrup

1 oz freshly squeezed lime juice

6 fresh mint leaves

6 oz sake

2 oz soda water

Directions
Place simple syrup, lime juice, and mint leaves in the bottom of a cocktail shaker and muddle the mint leaves with the bottom of a wooden spoon. Pour sake over the muddled mint leaves and fill the cocktail shaker with ice. Shake vigorously for 30 seconds. Fill a serving glass with fresh crushed ice. Strain and pour the cocktail into the serving glass. Top with soda water.

Vermouth Royale

Serving Size
Makes 1 drink

Ingredients
2 oz dry vermouth

1/2 oz crème de cassis

1/2 oz freshly squeezed lime juice

1/4 oz simple syrup

3 oz Prosecco

lemon peel for garnishing

Directions
Combine vermouth, crème de cassis, lime juice, and simple syrup in a mixing glass with ice. Stir for 30 to 45 seconds. Strain and pour the cocktail into a small stemmed serving glass. Top with Prosecco and garnish with a lemon peel.

Whiskey in a Teacup

Serving Size
Makes 1 drink

Ingredients
1 bag Earl Grey black tea

2 oz bourbon

1/2 oz freshly squeezed lemon juice

1/2 oz honey

1 lemon slice for garnishing

1 rosemary sprig for garnishing

Directions
Bring water in a medium pot or kettle to a boil. Steep bag of Earl Grey tea in boiling water. Once steeped, chill tea in the fridge for at least 1 hour. Combine cold tea, bourbon, lemon juice, and honey in a cocktail shaker with ice. Shake vigorously for 30 seconds. Strain and pour the cocktail into your fanciest tea cup and garnish with a lemon slice and rosemary sprig.

New York Sour

Serving Size
Makes 1 drink

Ingredients
2 oz rye whiskey or bourbon
1 oz freshly squeezed lemon juice
1/2 oz simple syrup
2 dashes Angostura bitters
1 oz red wine (Gamay or Pinot noir)
lemon peel for garnishing

Directions
Combine whiskey, lemon juice, simple syrup, and bitters in a cocktail shaker with ice. Shake vigorously for 30 to 45 seconds. Strain and pour the cocktail into a serving glass filled with fresh ice. Top with red wine and garnish with a lemon peel.

Brown Derby

Serving Size
Makes 1 drink

Ingredients
1 1/2 oz bourbon

1/2 oz honey

1 oz grapefruit juice

grapefruit peel for garnishing

Directions
Combine bourbon, honey, and grapefruit juice in a cocktail shaker with ice. Shake vigorously for 30 seconds. Rub grapefruit peel around the rim and inside of a serving glass. Strain and pour the cocktail into the serving glass. Squeeze grapefruit peel over the drink to release oils and then place the peel into drink.

Blood & Sand

Serving Size
Makes 1 drink

Ingredients
1 oz blended scotch

1/2 oz sweet vermouth

1/2 oz cherry liqueur

1/2 oz freshly squeezed orange juice

2 dashes Angostura bitters

1 maraschino cherry for garnishing

Directions
Combine scotch, sweet vermouth, cherry liqueur, orange juice, and bitters in a cocktail shaker and shake for 30 seconds. Strain and pour the cocktail into a serving glass. Spear a maraschino cherry with a cocktail pick (if you have one) and rest over the top of the glass.

Corpse Reviver No.1

Serving Size
Makes 1 drink

Ingredients
1 oz cognac

1 oz apple brandy

1/2 oz sweet vermouth

1 orange peel for garnishing

Directions
Combine cognac, apple brandy, and sweet vermouth in a mixing glass and stir for 60 seconds. Rub an orange peel around the rim and inside of a serving glass. Strain and pour the cocktail into the serving glass. Place the orange peel in the cocktail as garnish.

Rob Roy

Make sure to eat the maraschino cherry after you've finished the drink for one last burst of flavor.

Serving Size
Makes 1 drink

Ingredients
2 oz blended scotch

1 oz sweet vermouth

4 dashes Angostura bitters

1 maraschino cherry for garnishing

Directions
Combine scotch, sweet vermouth, and bitters in a mixing glass with ice. Stir vigorously for 30 to 45 seconds. Strain and pour the cocktail into a serving glass. Place the maraschino cherry in the cocktail as garnish.

The Sofía

Serving Size
Makes 1 drink

Ingredients
1/2 oz freshly squeezed lime juice

4 jalapeño pepper slices, seeds removed

2 oz mezcal

2 oz pineapple juice

1/2 oz agave syrup

1 pineapple wedge for garnishing

1 cilantro leaf for garnishing

Directions
Add lime juice and 2 jalapeño pepper slices to the bottom of a cocktail shaker. Muddle jalapeño pepper slices with the bottom of a wooden spoon. Combine mezcal, pineapple juice, and agave syrup in the cocktail shaker with lime juice and jalapeño pepper slices. Fill the cocktail shaker with ice and shake vigorously for 30 to 45 seconds. Fill a serving glass halfway with fresh ice. Strain and pour the cocktail into the serving glass. Place remaining jalapeño pepper slices in the cocktail. Place pineapple wedge and cilantro leaf on the rim of the glass as garnish.

Coconut & Rye Whiskey Soda

Serving Size
Makes 1 drink

Ingredients
6 oz coconut water

2 oz rye whiskey

5 oz coconut flavored soda water

1/2 oz freshly squeezed lime juice

1 lime slice for garnishing

mint leaves for garnishing

Directions
Pour coconut water into an ice cube tray and place in the freezer for 2 hours. Once frozen, fill a tall glass with coconut ice cubes. Pour rye whiskey over the ice. Top with coconut flavored soda water and lime juice. Place lime slice on the rim of the glass. Place mint leaves in the palm of your hand and smack with the palm of your other hand, like you are clapping. Place crushed mint leaves in the drink.